COLOSSIANS/ PHILEMON

New Life
in Christ

A Guided Discovery for Groups

LaVonne Neff

LOYOLAPRESS.
CHICAGO

LOYOLAPRESS.

3441 N. Ashland Avenue
Chicago, Illinois 60657
(800) 621-1008
WWW.LOYOLABOOKS.ORG

Nihil Obstat
Reverend John Lodge, S.S.L., S.T.D.
Censor Deputatus
August 31, 2002

Imprimatur
Most Reverend Raymond E. Goedert, M.A., S.T.L., J.C.L.
Vicar General
Archdiocese of Chicago
September 4, 2002

The *Nihil Obstat* and *Imprimatur* are official declarations that a book is free of doctrinal and moral error. No implication is contained therein that those who have granted the *Nihil Obstat* and *Imprimatur* agree with the content, opinions, or statements expressed. Nor do they assume any legal responsibility associated with publication.

The Scripture quotations contained herein are from the New Revised Standard Version Bible: Catholic Edition, copyright © 1993 and 1989 by the Division of Christian Education of the National Council of the Churches of Christ in the U.S.A. Used by permission. All rights reserved. Subheadings in Scripture quotations and line breaks in Colossians 1:15–20 have been added by LaVonne Neff.

The French text of the testament of Father Christian de Cherge (p. 31) can be found on the O.C.S.O. home page at www.ocso.org/testc-fr.htm. The translation here is by LaVonne Neff. An English version was published in *First Things* (August-September 1996): 21 and can be found at www.firstthings.com/ftissues/ft9608/opinion/cherge.html.

The excerpt from "Message to the People of Asia" and the excerpt from "On Evangelization in the Modern World" (p. 41) are from J. Neuner and J. Dupuis, eds., *The Christian Faith in the Doctrinal Documents of the Catholic Church* (New York: Alba House, 1990).

Interior design by Kay Hartmann/Communique Design
Illustration by Charise Mericle Harper

ISBN 0-8294-1486-X

Printed in the United States of America

03 04 05 06 07 Bang 10 9 8 7 6 5 4 3 2 1

Contents

How to Use This Guide

You might compare the Bible to a national park. The park is so large that you could spend months, even years, getting to know it. But a brief visit, if carefully planned, can be enjoyable and worthwhile. In a few hours you can drive through the park and pull over at a handful of sites. At each stop you can get out of the car, take a short trail through the woods, listen to the wind blowing through the trees, get a feel for the place.

In this booklet we will read two letters: an open letter from St. Paul (or one of his disciples) to the Christian communities at Colossae and Laodicea, and a personal letter from Paul to Philemon, a Christian coworker from Colossae. Because the letters are brief, we will be able to take a leisurely walk through them, thinking carefully about what we are reading and what it means for our lives today. While the letters are short, they give us much to reflect on, for they tell us a great deal about who Christ is and how Christ's followers should treat one another.

This guide provides everything you need to explore Colossians and Philemon in six discussions—or to do a six-part exploration on your own. The introduction on page 6 will prepare you to get the most out of your reading. The weekly sections provide explanations that highlight what the words of Scripture mean for us today. Equally important, each section supplies questions that will launch your group into fruitful discussion, helping you to both investigate the letter for yourself and to learn from one another. If you're using the booklet by yourself, the questions will spur your personal reflection.

Each discussion is meant to be a *guided discovery*.

Guided. None of us is equipped to read the Bible without help. We read the Bible *for* ourselves but not *by* ourselves. Scripture was written to be understood and applied in the community of faith. So each week "A Guide to the Reading," drawing on the work of both modern biblical scholars and Christian writers of the past, supplies background and explanations. The guide will help you grasp the message of Colossians and Philemon. Think of it as a friendly park ranger who points out noteworthy details and explains what you're looking at so you can appreciate things for yourself.

Discovery. The purpose is for *you* to interact with these New Testament letters. "Questions for Careful Reading" is a tool to help you dig into the text and examine it carefully. "Questions for Application" will help you consider what these words mean for your life here and now. Each week concludes with an "Approach to Prayer" section that helps you respond to God's word. Supplementary "Living Tradition" and "Saints in the Making" sections offer the thoughts and experiences of Christians past and present. By showing what these letters have meant to others, these sections will help you consider what they mean for you.

How long are the discussion sessions? We've assumed you will have about an hour and a half when you get together. If you have less time, you'll find that most of the elements can be shortened somewhat.

Is homework necessary? You will get the most out of your discussions if you read the weekly material and prepare your answers to the questions in advance of each meeting. If participants are not able to prepare, have someone read the "Guide to the Reading" sections aloud at the points where they appear.

What about leadership? If you happen to have a world-class biblical scholar in your group, by all means ask him or her to lead the discussions. In the absence of any professional Scripture scholars, or even accomplished amateur biblical scholars, you can still have a first-class Bible discussion. Choose two or three people to take turns as facilitators, and have everyone read "Suggestions for Bible Discussion Groups" (page 76) before beginning.

Does everyone need a guide? a Bible? Everyone in the group will need their own copy of this booklet. It contains the entire text of Colossians and Philemon, so a Bible is not absolutely necessary—but each participant will find it useful to have one. You should have at least one Bible on hand for your discussions. (See page 80 for recommendations.)

How do we get started? Before you begin, take a look at the suggestions for Bible discussion groups (page 76) or individuals (page 79).

Warm-Hearted but Clueless

You can't help liking these folks—the first readers of the letters to the Colossians and to Philemon. Among the believers of their day, the Colossian Christians have a widespread reputation for their faith in Christ and their love for one another. They're the kind of people who are interested in everything, who are willing to try anything, and who always have a good word for everybody. Philemon, one of their leaders, is known to be hospitable, strong in faith, and eager to encourage his fellow Christians. You get the feeling that if you wander into one of their church gatherings, they'll hug you, feed you, and give you a place to stay.

If there's one thing they're not, it's judgmental. In fact, they're so accepting of every new idea that they've fallen for quite a few strange ones—esoteric teachings about spirits and angels and visions, practices involving diet and rituals and self-denial. They really love Jesus, you see, and they think these beliefs and disciplines will make them even better Christians. Their non-Christian neighbors swear by these teachings and practices, and even though they aren't followers of Christ, they're deeply spiritual—after all, we're all God's children, aren't we?

The Colossians would be very comfortable—and even popular—in twenty-first-century America. Unfortunately, they are heading in a dangerous direction. The letter to the Colossians is an attempt to stop them before they slide into spiritual disaster.

Baby Christians. When the letters arrive, the Colossians have not been Christians for long—nobody has, in fact. Look at the chronology: Jesus of Nazareth was crucified about A.D. 30. During the next fifteen years, there were a lot of converts—three thousand in one day at Pentecost!—but nearly all of them lived in Palestine, and most were Jews. Around A.D. 46, Paul began his missionary journeys to largely Gentile cities in the eastern Roman Empire. The church in Colossae was formed only some ten years later.

The Acts of the Apostles—the scriptural book that tells the story of the first thirty years of Christianity—does not mention Colossae by name. Most likely the church there grew out of a series of public lectures Paul gave in Ephesus in the midfifties. Paul seems to have trained a number of associate evangelists, who then preached in other towns and established more churches than he could have done on his own. Paul's teaching in Ephesus "continued for two years," according to Acts 19:10, "so that all the residents of Asia, both Jews and Greeks, heard the word of the Lord." During that time, Epaphras apparently brought the new religion to Colossae (he is named in Colossians 1:7–8; 4:12–13; and Philemon 23).

If these two letters were written during a time when Paul was imprisoned in Ephesus, as some scholars think, the church at Colossae must have been only a year or two old when the letters arrived. If their setting is Paul's later imprisonment in Rome, the church was still only five or six years old. Imagine belonging to a religious movement that you first heard of less than a decade ago . . . that meets in private homes because it isn't exactly legal . . . that is based on stories told by a traveling missionary who left town shortly after forming the group . . . whose leaders are constantly in and out of jail . . . and whose reason for existence, Jesus, was executed a generation ago.

Difficult? You bet. Yet that was exactly the Colossians' situation. No wonder they sometimes seemed clueless.

Where the action was. Colossae was a small city in Asia Minor—the peninsula bounded by the Black Sea to the north, the Aegean to the west, and the Mediterranean to the south. Today the region makes up most of Turkey. Two thousand years ago, Asia Minor was a prosperous part of the Roman Empire.

Some fifty years before Paul's birth, his hometown of Tarsus in southern Asia Minor had celebrated the arrival of Queen Cleopatra, dressed as the goddess Venus, from Egypt. Marc Antony met her barge, and the rest is history.

Ephesus, named capital of Asia Minor by Caesar Augustus, was probably the fourth-largest city in the Roman Empire of Paul's day. Its gigantic buildings—whose ruins still take the breath away—included gymnasiums, baths, temples, a library, and a theater with seating for twenty-four thousand. According to one ancient tradition, Mary, the mother of Jesus, retired to the home of the apostle John in a village near Ephesus.

Tarsus and Ephesus were connected by a major trade route that ran through the Lycus River valley only a few miles from Colossae. Though in Paul's time only a small town, for many years Colossae had been known for its fine wool, and in its busy streets Greeks and Jews had mingled with merchants from all over the empire. The Colossians got to hear all sorts of new and fascinating ideas.

Letters from Paul? It was customary for letters to begin by identifying their senders, and these letters do exactly that: "Paul, a prisoner of Christ Jesus, and Timothy our brother," says verse 1 of the letter to Philemon, and verse 19 adds, "I, Paul, am writing this with my own hand." Similarly Colossians begins, "Paul, an apostle of Christ Jesus by the will of God, and Timothy our brother" (1:1) and ends, "I, Paul, write this greeting with my own hand" (4:18).

Paul was probably the best-known Christian of his day. Called the apostle to the Gentiles, he made three missionary journeys in twelve years and founded or visited churches in Palestine and Syria, Asia Minor and Greece, various Mediterranean islands, and Rome itself. Thirteen of the twenty-seven books of the New Testament claim his authorship.

Timothy, the son of a Greek father and a Jewish mother, met Paul in the late forties and several years later joined him in his travels through Asia Minor and Europe. A highly valued young coworker, Timothy must have spent a great deal of time talking theology with Paul, and his ideas may well be reflected in these letters, perhaps especially in Colossians 1, where the writers use *we* instead of *I*. Nevertheless, whenever *I* is used, it clearly means Paul, not Timothy. So the obvious conclusion is that Paul wrote the letters with Timothy's knowledge, agreement, and occasional collaboration.

Or someone else? The obvious conclusion, of course, is not always correct. Early in the nineteenth century, Scripture scholars began analyzing the ancient texts from new perspectives and with new information about the ancient world. Thanks to the patient examination of evidence by generations of scholars since then, new conclusions have developed about how, when, and by whom the books of the Bible were written.

At present, virtually all Scripture scholars continue to believe that Paul wrote the letter to Philemon. According to Raymond E. Brown, however, fewer than half think he wrote the letter to the Colossians. Most scholars hold that Colossians' unique vocabulary and style, its teachings regarding the Church, the type of false teachings it condemns, and the social milieu it describes all point to an author who lived a decade or two after Paul.

If these scholars are right, the author of the letter to the Colossians may have belonged to a group of Paul's disciples, probably in Ephesus. Having become Christians through Paul's teaching, these disciples knew his mind backward and forward. After his death, they continued to apply his wisdom to contemporary situations. It is possible that one of these "Paul specialists" used Colossae of the fifties or sixties as the setting for a letter written in Paul's name that addressed problems facing a number of churches in the seventies or eighties.

Would this mean that the letter to the Colossians is a forgery? Not at all. Ancient authors often preferred to associate their writings with well-known individuals or schools of thought rather than with their own names, and the early Church readily accepted Colossians as inspired Scripture because of its profound theology, practical wisdom, and clear link to Paul's teachings.

Whoever actually put pen to papyrus, we are going to call him *Paul* and interpret the letter as though it was written to the Christians in Colossae shortly after their conversion. This is not taking sides in the discussion. It is just a whole lot easier than repeatedly writing "the author of the letter to the Colossians"!

Why is Paul worried? Paul has never visited Colossae, and he can't come now because he's in prison. He has been hearing reports, however, that worry him. He fears that the Colossian Christians may be falling for some teachings that threaten to compromise their Christian faith. It's a constant struggle, Paul thinks. Heaven knows he's had trouble keeping the churches in Galatia and Corinth on the straight and narrow. But the Colossians! Can't anybody remember their priorities anymore?

Sometimes when we read Scripture, the stories seem to come from another planet. The world of the Colossian Christians, by contrast, sounds very familiar: multinational businesses, excellent communications, frequent long-distance travel, pervasive interest in spirituality. The Roman Empire of the first century is an exciting time and place to be alive. It's possible, for example, to worship the emperor, the mother-goddess Cybele, the many-breasted Artemis, and the terrible Zeus all in the same week. Even Judaism, though strict and exclusive in Jerusalem, relaxes as it leaves its home turf and begins to mix it up—ever so discreetly—with other spiritualities. If the Colossians had had megabookstores, they would have enjoyed our entire range of religion titles: a selection of books on the traditional religions, of course, but also books on angels, spirits, philosophies, exercises, diets, prophets, horoscopes, numerology, moon rituals, witchcraft, revelations, prophecies . . .

Stop! Paul shouts, his hands over his ears. These things all look impressive—but they aren't Christianity! At best, they are weak imitations, mere shadows of Christ. Don't listen to people who tell you there's something wrong with you unless you do things their way. Don't believe teachers who say anything is more important than Christ. Do some theology, my friends! Learn who Christ is! Only then will you know true wisdom.

What does this have to do with daily life? Paul's letters generally start with theology and end with behavior, and Colossians is no exception. Paul begins by preaching the gospel— telling his readers who Christ is and what Christ has done for them, laying out a clear contrast between Christian teachings and the spiritual grab bag they've been rummaging in. Once he has laid this foundation, he turns to the stuff of everyday life. After listing behaviors that Christians should avoid as well as behaviors they should adopt, he offers general instructions on how Christians should relate to the members of their households.

And that brings us to the tiny letter to Philemon. Though it was probably written before the letter to the Colossians, we are saving it for last because it is such a wonderful example of how the theology and practical instructions of the letter to the Colossians play out in real life.

The letter to Philemon is so short—only twenty-five verses and 460 words in the translation we are using—that it isn't divided into chapters. It skips past the usual theological section and cuts right to the chase. You can read the whole letter in a minute or two. Philemon himself, however, must have spent a lot more time with it than that. The letter asks him to do something he would have found extremely difficult: to forgive his dishonest runaway slave, Onesimus ("Oh-NESS-uh-muss"), and welcome him as a brother.

Why was this small personal letter included in Scripture? Maybe because of its clear call to show faith by action. Maybe because it offers such an engagingly personal picture of Paul reconciling two Christians. And just maybe because of the direction Onesimus's life took after he was freed.

Early in the second century, the bishop of Ephesus was a man named Onesimus. No one knows for sure if he was Philemon's slave, but it's certainly possible. Some scholars have suggested that Bishop Onesimus was the editor who first gathered and published Paul's letters—including the tiny one that, to him, was most important of all. It is intriguing to think that Philemon, by agreeing to Paul's request, may have played a role in creating the New Testament.

Is there any connection between Christ's superiority over all the competing spiritualities (Colossians) to the way a Christian ought to run his household (Colossians and Philemon)? Paul seems to think so. As you read the two letters, look for the links between his teachings about Christ and his advice for daily life. Does it matter that through Christ, God reconciles to himself all things (Colossians 1:20)? Does it make a difference that God made us alive with him, forgiving our sins (Colossians 2:13)? Is this "just theology," or is it profound truth about God's action toward us— truth that, if we really believe it and apply it to our lives, changes all our human relationships?

LORD OF THE COSMOS

Questions to Begin

15 minutes
Use a question or two to get warmed up for the reading.

---

1 Have you ever received a really memorable thank-you letter (or e-mail or phone call)? What made it so special?

---

2 Do you know someone—or have you heard of someone—who deserves to be called a saint? What is saintly about him or her?

---

3 What is your favorite hymn? Why do you like it?

Opening the Bible

5 minutes
Read the passage aloud. Let individuals take turns reading paragraphs.

The Reading: Colossians 1:1–23

Faith, Love, and Hope at Colossae

1 Paul, an apostle of Christ Jesus by the will of God, and Timothy our brother,

2 To the saints and faithful brothers and sisters in Christ in Colossae:

Grace to you and peace from God our Father.

3 In our prayers for you we always thank God, the Father of our Lord Jesus Christ, 4 for we have heard of your faith in Christ Jesus and of the love that you have for all the saints, 5 because of the hope laid up for you in heaven. You have heard of this hope before in the word of the truth, the gospel 6 that has come to you. Just as it is bearing fruit and growing in the whole world, so it has been bearing fruit among yourselves from the day you heard it and truly comprehended the grace of God. 7 This you learned from Epaphras, our beloved fellow servant. He is a faithful minister of Christ on your behalf, 8 and he has made known to us your love in the Spirit.

Our Prayer for You

9 For this reason, since the day we heard it, we have not ceased praying for you and asking that you may be filled with the knowledge of God's will in all spiritual wisdom and understanding, 10 so that you may lead lives worthy of the Lord, fully pleasing to him, as you bear fruit in every good work and as you grow in the knowledge of God. 11 May you be made strong with all the strength that comes from his glorious power, and may you be prepared to endure everything with patience, while joyfully 12 giving thanks to the Father, who has enabled you to share in the inheritance of the saints in the light. 13 He has rescued us from the power of darkness and transferred us into the kingdom of his beloved Son, 14 in whom we have redemption, the forgiveness of sins.

A Hymn to Christ

15 He is the image of the invisible God,
   the firstborn of all creation;

16 for in him all things in heaven and on earth were created,
  things visible and invisible,
  whether thrones or dominions or rulers or powers—
  all things have been created through him and for him.

17 He himself is before all things,
  and in him all things hold together.
18 He is the head of the body, the church;
  he is the beginning, the firstborn from the dead,
  so that he might come to have first place in everything.

19 For in him all the fullness of God was pleased to dwell,
    20 and through him God was pleased to reconcile to himself
    all things,
  whether on earth or in heaven,
  by making peace through the blood of his cross.

The Gospel in a Nutshell

21 And you who were once estranged and hostile in mind, doing evil deeds, 22 he has now reconciled in his fleshly body through death, so as to present you holy and blameless and irreproachable before him— 23 provided that you continue securely established and steadfast in the faith, without shifting from the hope promised by the gospel that you heard, which has been proclaimed to every creature under heaven.

10 minutes
Choose questions according to your interest and time.

1 Paul addresses this letter "to the saints and faithful brothers and sisters." Who does he mean by *saints* (verses 2, 4, 12)? How does he describe their character (verses 4–8)? What virtues might they still lack (verses 9–12)?

2 *Hope* is mentioned three times in this reading (verses 5, 23). What do Christians hope for?

3 *Gospel* means "good news." In this reading, what is the good news that "has been proclaimed to every creature under heaven" (verse 23)? What is the connection between hope and the gospel?

4 The hymn (verses 15–20) includes several repetitions or parallel ideas. See how many you can find. What word or phrase is repeated most often? What is the effect of this repetition?

5 What lines in the hymn make it clear that Christ has a unique relationship to God?

A Guide to the Reading

If participants have not read this section already, read it aloud. Otherwise go on to "Questions for Application."

1:1–8. My e-mail program puts four important pieces of information at the beginning of every message: *From, Date, To,* and *Subject.* Letters in Paul's day typically began in a similar way: first they identified the sender, then they named the recipients, and finally they politely wished the recipients well. Paul follows the formula, but with a twist all his own. Instead of the usual *Greetings,* he chooses a word that in Greek sounds almost like it: *Grace,* and then he adds the standard Jewish salutation: *Peace.* Right at the top of the page, Paul brings Jews and Greeks together in Christ.

First-century writers had a lovely custom of beginning the body of their letters with thanksgiving. Though Paul doesn't know many of the Colossians personally, he is thankful for the good things he's heard about them. They are strong in what would come to be called the theological virtues: faith, hope, and love. In fact, Paul calls them "saints"—"holy ones," in some translations—people who have been set apart for a special purpose. Since all baptized Christians have been set apart to love and serve God, our parishes are full of saints!

1:9–14. Ancient letters often included prayers. Paul prays that the Colossians will receive knowledge and strength, tough virtues that these lovable new Christians were a bit short of. He then (in verses 13–14) uses words they may have spoken at their baptisms only a few years earlier: God has forgiven their sins, rescued them from "the power of darkness," and redeemed them—that is, paid to free them from slavery. Thanks to the Father, they now live "in the light," in "the kingdom of his beloved Son."

1:15–20. This is probably a hymn that early Christians—including the Colossians—used in their liturgies. The hymn's picture of Jesus is magnificent. The Catechism sums it up like this, "It is in Christ, 'the image of the invisible God,' that man has been created 'in the image and likeness' of the Creator. It is in Christ, Redeemer and Savior, that the divine image, disfigured in man by the first sin, has been restored to its original beauty and ennobled by the grace of God" (*Catechism of the Catholic Church,* section 1701).

You can get this vision of Christ in, of all places, the hymn's prepositions. Paul pictures a universe that is drenched in

Christ. Creation is *in* him, *through* him, and *for* him. "*In* him all things hold together" (emphasis added). *In* him dwells the fullness of God. *Through* him God reconciles all things. Scripture scholar F. F. Bruce writes, "For those who have been redeemed by Christ, the universe has no ultimate terrors; they know that their Redeemer is also creator, ruler, and goal of all."

The Colossians knew all this—they sang the hymn, after all—but the words had become so familiar that they had lost their power to shock. Just as we can slide through a Mass without giving much thought to what is really happening on the altar, the Colossians could repeat the outrageous idea that the fullness of God was pleased to dwell in a Palestinian carpenter's son—and then go out and look for God in other places.

Paul would have understood Annie Dillard's cry in *Teaching a Stone to Talk:* "Does anyone have the foggiest idea what sort of power we so blithely invoke?"

Paul clearly knew that power, and he wanted everyone else to know too. The Christ we worship is no less than the creator of "all things in heaven and on earth." He is the one who reconciles heaven and earth to God. He is the cosmic Christ, the Lord of the universe, the one who is "before all things," the one in whom "all things hold together."

1:21–23. No way is this Christ just a local god, Paul says; the good news about him has gone out to the whole world (see also verse 6). Paul's words just before the hymn suggested baptism. His words here suggest the Eucharist. Christ has made peace "through the blood of his cross"; he has reconciled us "in his fleshly body through death." Christ's body and blood have become food for our journey of faith and hope. The journey may be long and hard, Paul implies, but the result is worth everything. Don't wimp out now!

Questions for Application

40 minutes
Choose questions according to your interest and time.

---

1 *Thanksgiving* is one of Paul's favorite themes. Reread verses 3–5 and 11–12. What are you thankful for this week?

---

2 Tell about a time when you prayed for someone or when someone prayed for you. How were your prayers answered? Was there any change in your relationship with the other person?

---

3 How old were you when you first understood the gospel? What difference has this good news made in your life?

---

4 If Christ is Lord of the cosmos, where is the evidence of his power? What gives you a sense of awe in his presence? Where do you see his power at work?

5 God gives power to "endure everything with patience" and thankfulness. How do you tell the difference between what you can—and should—change and what you must endure? How can you be strengthened with God's strength?

6 In verse 23 Paul emphasizes the need to continue in the faith, to be persistent in one's spiritual life. How do the sacraments help us to persist? What practical help do they give for our everyday lives?

7 Is anyone praying for your spiritual growth as Paul and Timothy prayed for the Colossians'? Are you praying for someone else to grow in Christ? If you are in a small group, would you be interested in agreeing to pray for one another by name between meetings?

It is in small groups that people can get close enough to know each other, to care and share, to challenge and support, to confide and confess, to forgive and be forgiven, to laugh and weep together, to be accountable to each other, to watch over each other, and to grow together.

Gilbert Bilezikian, *Community 101*

Approach to Prayer

15 minutes
Use this approach—or create your own!

◆ Pray the Hymn to Christ from
this week's Scripture reading,
using "you" instead of "he."
Then end with a Glory to the
Father.

You are the image of the invisible
God,
the firstborn of all creation;
for in you all things in heaven
and on earth were created,
things visible and invisible,
whether thrones or dominions
or rulers or powers—
all things have been created
through you and for you.

You are before all things,
and in you all things hold
together.
You are the head of the body, the
church;
You are the beginning, the
firstborn from the dead,
so that you might come to
have first place in
everything.

For in you all the fullness of God
was pleased to dwell,
and through you God was
pleased to reconcile to
himself all things,
whether on earth or in heaven,
by making peace through the
blood of your cross.

A Living Tradition

Radical Tunes

This section is a supplement for individual reading.

Christians from Jewish families were familiar with the scriptural Psalms, while Gentile Christians would have known various hymns to pagan gods. As converts to Christianity, both groups continued to sing. "With gratitude in your hearts," Paul wrote to the Colossians, "sing psalms, hymns, and spiritual songs to God" (3:16).

Half a century later, Pliny the Younger, a governor in Asia Minor, asked the Roman emperor Trajan for advice on how to deal with followers of this new religion. What did Christians do? According to Pliny, "they were in the habit of meeting regularly before dawn and singing a hymn to Christ, as to a god."

What might these early Christians have been singing? Possibly Colossians 1:15–20, the hymn we are looking at this week. Another beautiful "hymn to Christ, as to a god" is found in Philippians 2:5–11:

> Let the same mind be in you that was in Christ Jesus,
> who, though he was in the form of God,
>   did not regard equality with God
>   as something to be exploited,
> but emptied himself,
>   taking the form of a slave. . . .
> Therefore God also highly exalted him
>   and gave him the name
>   that is above every name,
> so that at the name of Jesus
>   every knee should bend,
>   in heaven and on earth and under the earth,
> and every tongue should confess
>   that Jesus Christ is Lord,
>   to the glory of God the Father.

Two thousand years later, these early hymns seem inspiring—but tame. In fact, they were anything but. To their Jewish neighbors, identifying Jesus of Nazareth with God was blasphemous. To the Roman peace officers, calling Jesus (instead of the emperor) "Lord" was seditious. Singing hymns to Christ in the first century was to identify with an extremely radical faith.

WORTH THE PRICE

Questions to Begin

15 minutes
Use a question or two to get warmed up for the reading.

1 "It is just so unfair." Have you said this recently? What about?

2 Is it ever okay to be proud? What are you most proud of?
❑ achievements
❑ beauty
❑ brains
❑ family
❑ moral standards
❑ nationality
❑ net worth
❑ physical strength
❑ possessions
❑ power/influence
❑ relationships
❑ religion
❑ social status
❑ _____

3 When does pride become disgusting—or dangerous?

Opening the Bible

5 minutes
Read the passage aloud. Let individuals take turns reading
paragraphs.

The Reading: 2 Corinthians 11:21–33; Colossians 1:23–2:3

Paul's Resumé

2 Corinthians 11:21 Whatever anyone dares to boast of—I am speaking as
a fool—I also dare to boast of that. 22 Are they Hebrews? So am I. Are
they Israelites? So am I. Are they descendants of Abraham? So am I.
23 Are they ministers of Christ? I am talking like a madman—I am a
better one: with far greater labors, far more imprisonments, with
countless floggings, and often near death. 24 Five times I have received
from the Jews the forty lashes minus one. 25 Three times I was beaten
with rods. Once I received a stoning. Three times I was shipwrecked;
for a night and a day I was adrift at sea; 26 on frequent journeys,
in danger from rivers, danger from bandits, danger from my own
people, danger from Gentiles, danger in the city, danger in the
wilderness, danger at sea, danger from false brothers and sisters;
27 in toil and hardship, through many a sleepless night, hungry and
thirsty, often without food, cold and naked. 28 And, besides other
things, I am under daily pressure because of my anxiety for all the
churches. 29 Who is weak, and I am not weak? Who is made to
stumble, and I am not indignant?

30 If I must boast, I will boast of the things that show my
weakness. 31 The God and Father of the Lord Jesus (blessed be he
forever!) knows that I do not lie. 32 In Damascus, the governor under
King Aretas guarded the city of Damascus in order to seize me, 33 but
I was let down in a basket through a window in the wall, and escaped
from his hands.

The Mystery

Colossians 1:23 I, Paul, became a servant of this gospel.

24 I am now rejoicing in my sufferings for your sake, and in my
flesh I am completing what is lacking in Christ's afflictions for the
sake of his body, that is, the church. 25 I became its servant according
to God's commission that was given to me for you, to make the word
of God fully known, 26 the mystery that has been hidden throughout
the ages and generations but has now been revealed to his saints.
27 To them God chose to make known how great among the Gentiles
are the riches of the glory of this mystery, which is Christ in you, the

hope of glory. [28] It is he whom we proclaim, warning everyone and teaching everyone in all wisdom, so that we may present everyone mature in Christ. [29] For this I toil and struggle with all the energy that he powerfully inspires within me.

[2:1] For I want you to know how much I am struggling for you, and for those in Laodicea, and for all who have not seen me face to face. [2] I want their hearts to be encouraged and united in love, so that they may have all the riches of assured understanding and have the knowledge of God's mystery, that is, Christ himself, [3] in whom are hidden all the treasures of wisdom and knowledge.

10 minutes
Choose questions according to your interest and time.

1 Paul was often in danger of religious persecution. What other kinds of danger did he face? Which dangers would have been most distressing to him?

2 Why does Paul consider his suffering worthwhile? Why does he rejoice? Does Paul enjoy suffering?

3 As a "servant of the gospel," what are Paul's duties? For whom does he work? What are his goals?

4 The word *mystery* is used here three times. What is the mystery? Why do you think Paul calls it a mystery? Is it still a mystery today?

5 What kind of knowledge, wisdom, and understanding does Paul want his readers to gain? What are the results of this wisdom?

A Guide to the Reading

If participants have not read this section already, read it aloud. Otherwise go on to "Questions for Application."

2 Corinthians 11:21–33. Corinth is in Greece, a long way from Colossae, but this excerpt from Paul's second letter to the Corinthians helps us understand why Paul writes about his suffering. It also clearly shows what kinds of suffering Paul endured.

"Who does he think he is?" It's a natural response when someone has just criticized you or cut down one of your cherished beliefs, and it's probably what the Christians in Corinth were saying about Paul when they heard what he'd been saying about them.

Paul, still working in Ephesus, did not like what he was hearing about some of the teachers in Corinth. Not only were they subverting his theology, they were challenging him personally. "Super-apostles," he scornfully called them. "Take a look at my resumé and see if they measure up."

And what a resumé Paul has! He doesn't list his university degrees, professional achievements, or prestigious awards. Instead, he sends them his entire police record along with a detailed account of natural disasters and human perfidy he has experienced. What gives Paul the right to challenge other religious teachers? Love—love so strong that he is willing to sacrifice everything for Christ and Christ's followers.

Colossians 1:23–24. The situation in Colossae is similar. Again Paul is worried about heretical teachers infiltrating the Christian church. But whereas Paul knew the Corinthians personally, he had never even visited Colossae. How could he expect the Colossians to listen to him, an unknown old man in prison? "I guess I'll just have to send them my resumé," he must have said to himself. "I think this time I'll spell it out before they disappoint me."

It's not hard to believe that a person might accept suffering on behalf of someone they love. But how can Paul rejoice in his suffering?—and in what way can he be "completing what is lacking in Christ's afflictions"? Hasn't this letter already said that through Christ's blood, "God was pleased to reconcile to himself *all* things" (1:20; emphasis added)?

Paul is not suggesting that Christ didn't do enough. Later in Colossians, in fact, he will argue against teachers who try to add anything to Christ's gospel. Paul may be expressing his mystical unity with Christ by identifying his own sufferings with those of his Lord. His remark may reflect a belief among some Jews of his day that a certain number of trials must occur before the messianic age begins. For Paul, the old era has been destroyed and a new era has begun with Christ. But until Christ's return, we live in an intermediate time of suffering. Paul can rejoice in his suffering because (1) he sees it as part of the trials that will bring in the Messiah's kingdom, (2) he is thrilled to see the gospel being preached throughout the Roman Empire and he accepts suffering as part of the package, and (3) he knows that the "power of darkness" has already been sentenced to death and the "kingdom of [God's] beloved Son" is at hand (Colossians 1:13).

Colossians 1:25–2:3. If Paul were reading this book over your shoulder, he'd be pretty annoyed by now. "Why all this talk about Paul?" he'd ask. "It's not about me; it's about Christ." All his hard work and struggles are for one purpose only: to reveal Christ to the world. N. T. Wright suggests that "to make the word of God fully known" (1:25) is too tame a translation. For Paul, the word of God is a power let loose in the world, a long-hidden mystery only now being revealed.

The Roman Empire swarmed with "mystery religions" whose initiates, after following secret rituals, expected to gain hidden knowledge. By contrast, God's mystery—Christ in us, the hope of glory—is now open to the entire universe. Paul teaches *everyone* so that *everyone* can grow to maturity in Christ (1:28), even including "*all* who have not seen me face to face" (2:1, emphasis added). The mystery is Christ himself—the cosmic Christ at the heart of the universe as well as the personal Christ in the hearts of all who believe in him; Christ among the Gentiles as well as among the Jews; Christ whose presence gives hope; Christ the source of all wisdom and knowledge; Christ who reveals God; Christ who *is* God. Christ and Christ's people—these are Paul's reasons for joyful suffering.

Questions for Application

40 minutes
Choose questions according to your interest and time.

1 Paul often writes about rejoicing. Reread Colossians 1:24. What are you rejoicing about this week?

2 Paul knew what God wanted him to do, and he didn't let anything stand in the way of accomplishing his mission. Do you have a God-given mission in life? (It doesn't have to be religious.) What are you willing to sacrifice in order to carry it out?

3 Do you know anyone personally who has suffered because of his or her faith in Christ? Why was this person willing to suffer? How has he or she inspired you?

4 Think about a time of suffering in your life. What gave you the courage to go through it? If you could live that part of your life over again, would you avoid the suffering?

5 Read Matthew 5:44–48, Luke 23:34, and Acts 7:59–60. Can you forgive someone who causes you to suffer? What might be the result of forgiveness in your life and in the other person's?

6 Paul speaks about being "mature in Christ." What are the characteristics of a "baby" Christian? a child? an adolescent? an adult? What stage do you think you're in? What do you need to do in order to keep growing? Mention specific actions you could take.

7 The mystery at the heart of Paul's message is "Christ in you, the hope of glory" (Colossians 1:27). As a Christian, what is your deepest hope? To what extent is this hope a wish, and to what extent is it a certainty? Does its fulfillment depend on you or on God?

Whenever we are with people who suffer, it frequently becomes evident that there is very little we can do to help them other than be present to them, walk with them as the Lord walks with us. The reason this is so frustrating is that we like to be "fixers."

Cardinal Joseph Bernardin, *The Gift of Peace*

Approach to Prayer

15 minutes
Use one of these approaches—or create your own!

◆ Let someone read the invitation in Hebrews 4:14–16. Then individuals may ask for prayers for people who are suffering any kind of pain, illness, or difficulty. After each request, all respond, "Lord, have mercy." End with an Our Father.

◆ Pray together this prayer attributed to the sixteenth-century Spanish saint Ignatius Loyola:

Eternal Word, only begotten Son
of God,
Teach us to be generous.
Teach us to serve you as you
deserve:
to give and not to count the
cost,
to fight and not to heed the
wounds,
to toil and not to seek for rest,
to labor and not to ask for
reward
save the knowledge that we do
your will.

Saints in the Making

A Martyr Forgives

This section is a supplement for individual reading.

In 1996 Father Christian de Cherge, the superior of a Trappist monastery in Algeria, was kidnapped and executed along with six other monks. A terrorist group claimed responsibility. Two years earlier, Father de Cherge had sent his family an amazing "last testament," to be opened at his death. Here are some excerpts:

I have lived long enough to know I partake in the evil that seems, alas, to prevail in the world, and even in the evil that may blindly strike me. I would like, when the time comes, to be conscious long enough to beg forgiveness of God and of my brothers in humanity, as well as to wholeheartedly forgive my attacker. . . .

I do not see how I could rejoice if the people I love are indiscriminately accused of my murder. It is too high a price for what may be called the "grace of martyrdom" to owe it to an Algerian, whoever he might be, especially if he thinks he is acting in faithfulness to what he believes to be Islam. I know . . . the caricatures of Islam that a certain kind of idealism encourages. It is too easy to ease one's conscience by identifying this religious path with the fanaticism of its extremists.

Algeria and Islam . . . are my body and my soul. I have frequently and openly proclaimed—right here in Algeria, and with the respect of believing Muslims—that so often I find in Islam a direct line to the gospel I learned at my mother's knees, my very first church. . . . [In death,] at long last, my all-consuming curiosity will be given free rein. There I will be able, God willing, to immerse my gaze in that of the Father in order to contemplate, with him, his Islamic children just as he sees them, all radiant with Christ's glory, the fruit of his passion, gifted by the Spirit whose secret joy will always be to create communion and to re-create likeness, while enjoying the differences. . . .

And you, my last-moment friend, who will not have known what you were doing. Yes, this thank-you . . . and this "A-Dieu" [are] intended for you. May we be permitted to meet one another as "good thieves" in Paradise, if it pleases God, the Father of us both.

USELESS SPIRITUALITY

Questions to Begin

15 minutes
Use a question or two to get warmed up for the reading.

1 Where are you on the Skepticism Scale?
  ❑ If I can't see it, hear it, touch it, or smell it, I don't believe it.
  ❑ I believe that an unseen world exists, but I've never been in touch with it myself.
  ❑ I've had contact with angels, spirits, or the dead a time or two.
  ❑ I frequently commune with beings from another dimension.
  ❑ I personally know someone who has been kidnapped by an extraterrestrial.

2 What is the strangest thing you (or someone you know) ever gave up for Lent? Was it a helpful experience?

3 Tell about a time when you were forgiven even though you were clearly in the wrong. How did you feel?

5 minutes
Read the passage aloud. Let individuals take turns reading paragraphs.

The Reading: Colossians 2:4–23

Keep Up the Good Work

4 I am saying this so that no one may deceive you with plausible arguments. 5 For though I am absent in body, yet I am with you in spirit, and I rejoice to see your morale and the firmness of your faith in Christ.

6 As you therefore have received Christ Jesus the Lord, continue to live your lives in him, 7 rooted and built up in him and established in the faith, just as you were taught, abounding in thanksgiving.

The Reality: Life in Christ

8 See to it that no one takes you captive through philosophy and empty deceit, according to human tradition, according to the elemental spirits of the universe, and not according to Christ. 9 For in him the whole fullness of deity dwells bodily, 10 and you have come to fullness in him, who is the head of every ruler and authority. 11 In him also you were circumcised with a spiritual circumcision, by putting off the body of the flesh in the circumcision of Christ; 12 when you were buried with him in baptism, you were also raised with him through faith in the power of God, who raised him from the dead. 13 And when you were dead in trespasses and the uncircumcision of your flesh, God made you alive together with him, when he forgave us all our trespasses, 14 erasing the record that stood against us with its legal demands. He set this aside, nailing it to the cross. 15 He disarmed the rulers and authorities and made a public example of them, triumphing over them in it.

The Shadow: Human Commands

16 Therefore do not let anyone condemn you in matters of food and drink or of observing festivals, new moons, or sabbaths. 17 These are only a shadow of what is to come, but the substance belongs to Christ. 18 Do not let anyone disqualify you, insisting on self-abasement and worship of angels, dwelling on visions, puffed up without cause by a human way of thinking, 19 and not holding fast to

the head, from whom the whole body, nourished and held together by its ligaments and sinews, grows with a growth that is from God.

20 If with Christ you died to the elemental spirits of the universe, why do you live as if you still belonged to the world? Why do you submit to regulations, 21 "Do not handle, Do not taste, Do not touch"? 22 All these regulations refer to things that perish with use; they are simply human commands and teachings. 23 These have indeed an appearance of wisdom in promoting self-imposed piety, humility, and severe treatment of the body, but they are of no value in checking self-indulgence.

10 minutes
Choose questions according to your interest and time.

1 What has Paul been saying to his readers to prevent them from being deceived? (Look again at last week's reading.) Does Paul give any indication that his readers are being deceived or are doing anything wrong? Why is he so worried?

2 What does baptism have in common with death and resurrection?

3 What ideas and beings are opposed to Christ? Why is Christ superior to them?

4 This reading contrasts Christ's forgiveness with the condemnation and disqualification that are coming from others. What does Christ get rid of? What do these others insist upon?

5 Notice how often Paul says "in Christ" ("in him") or "with Christ" ("with him"). How is being "in Christ" different from belonging "to the world"?

A Guide to the Reading

*If participants have not read this section already, read it aloud.
Otherwise go on to "Questions for Application."*

2:4–7. In the reading for week 1, Paul reminded the Colossians
that Christ is Lord of the entire cosmos. In the reading for week 2,
he assured them that he, Paul, loves them enough to suffer for
them. Now he is ready to attack the teachings that are beginning
to seduce them. Paul warns his Colossian friends, but he does not
scold them. Christ has made a huge difference in your lives ever
since you were baptized, he writes. Keep on being faithful and
grateful to him, just as you were taught.

    2:8–23. It's impossible to know just what the captivating
teachings were. Some scholars think they were based on Judaism.
Paul's description certainly has Jewish elements: circumcision,
new-moon festivals, sabbaths, food laws. Others point out elements
of other religions: philosophy, human tradition, "elemental spirits"
(possibly heavenly bodies or other entities that supposedly ruled
the world). Most likely the false teachers were cobbling together
features of various spiritual traditions.

    Asia Minor, the Roman province that included Colossae,
was an incredibly religious place. A few years earlier, in Ephesus,
Paul had accidentally triggered a riot by devotees of the goddess
Artemis (see Acts 19:23–41). In Lystra, to the east, mania of rock-
star intensity broke out around Paul and his companion Barnabas
when the townspeople mistook them for the Greek gods Zeus and
Hermes (Acts 14:8–20). Hierapolis, Colossae's near neighbor, was
a center for a mystery religion devoted to the mother goddess
Cybele. Many cities had active Jewish synagogues. A spiritual
philosophy (later called *Gnosticism*) was developing that
emphasized esoteric knowledge, the goodness of spirit, and the
evil of matter. Faced with an excess of choice, most people
practiced *syncretism*—they mixed together various sets of beliefs
and rituals to produce something that they hoped would work for
them, rather as many Americans do today.

    In Colossae, Raymond E. Brown concludes, the false
teachers "combined belief in Christ with Jewish and Pagan ideas
to shape a hierarchical system of heavenly beings in which Christ
was subordinated to angelic powers to whom worship was due."
Whatever the specifics, Paul insists, the choice is clear: you are
either with Christ or with the world. Here are your options:

- ◆ Christ offers rescue from the power of darkness (1:13); the other teachers want to take you captive (2:8).
- ◆ Christ offers "all the treasures of wisdom and knowledge" (2:3); the other teachers give "an appearance of wisdom" (2:23) that is actually "empty deceit" (2:8).
- ◆ In Christ is the "fullness of deity" (2:9); the other teachers offer "human tradition" (2:8).
- ◆ Christ offers spiritual nourishment and growth (2:19); the programs offered by the other teachers "are of no value in checking self-indulgence" (2:23).
- ◆ And anyway, Christ created and rules "every ruler and authority" (2:10)—including the other teachers and the spiritual powers they represent.

Don't be taken in by the false teachers, Paul pleads. They will only deceive you (2:4), enslave you (2:8), condemn you (2:16), disqualify you (2:18), or regulate you (2:20–21).

How could faithful, loving Christians ever fall for teachers who wanted to mess up their lives so thoroughly? Was it only because of their dangerous mixture of curiosity and naïveté? Or were they feeling frustration and guilt, worry that they were not completely forgiven for their former lives? No doubt they sometimes relapsed into the kinds of behavior they had hoped to put behind them—after all, they were human. And suddenly along came these self-help gurus "with plausible arguments" saying, "We know how you can become exactly the people you want to be."

But, Paul warns, their prescriptions—no matter how appealing—ultimately won't get you where you want to go. There's a better way. When you were baptized, you died to your sins. God forgave you and gave you new life. Now hold on to Christ, continue to live in him, and watch your new life develop. You don't need to try a new spirituality. You need to put down roots in Christ, take nourishment from one another, and allow God to guide your growth.

If this sounds vague, keep reading. In later chapters Paul will give pointed suggestions on how Christians should—and should not—live out their faith.

Questions for Application

40 minutes
Choose questions according to your interest and time.

1 Reread verses 5–7. What are you rejoicing about—or thankful for—this week?

2 Nowadays religious teachers are all over the media. How can you tell if their ideas are sound? What do you need to know about these teachers in order to avoid being deceived?

3 Paul wants the Colossians to be "rooted and built up" in Christ. What practices help faith develop roots and grow? For ideal spiritual growth, what do you need to do daily? Is God nudging you to make some growth-producing practice more regular in your life?

4 Paul says that some spiritual practices can separate people from Christ. Is it possible for a spiritual discipline to help one person grow but to separate another person from Christ? What would make the difference? How can you be sure that your own disciplines help to establish you in the faith (2:7)?

5 What has God done for you that no human can possibly do? First look for responses suggested by the reading, and then see if you can extend the list.

6 Our human brothers and sisters are the "ligaments and sinews" that nourish us and hold us together in Christ (2:19). How have you been nourished by a fellow Christian? How have you given nourishment to others? What can you do during the next seven days that will bring nourishment to someone else?

The facilitator should ensure that everyone in the group has an opportunity to share to the extent that they wish to do so (no coercion, please).

Margaret Silf, *Inner Compass*

Approach to Prayer

15 minutes
Use one of these approaches—or create your own!

◆ Christ is the heart of Paul's life. For Paul, life began when he met Christ on the Damascus Road and was baptized into Christ.

Sing as much of "Amazing Grace" as the group can remember. Then sit quietly for a few moments, meditating on the difference Christ makes in your life. Spontaneous prayers of praise and thanksgiving would be appropriate. End with a Glory to the Father.

◆ Pray together this thirteenth-century prayer by St. Richard, Bishop of Chichester, England:

We thank you, Lord Jesus Christ,
for all the benefits you have
        given us,
and for all the pains and insults
        you have borne for us.
Most merciful redeemer, friend,
        and brother,
may we know you more clearly,
love you more dearly,
and follow you more nearly
day by day.

A Living Tradition

Other Paths to God?

This section is a supplement for individual reading.

Like twenty-first-century Americans, first-century Colossians were in constant contact with a whole variety of religious traditions. Most Colossians, including many Christians, took whatever suited them out of the spiritual stew, flavoring their worship with ideas and rituals from other religions. St. Paul objected strenuously—yet throughout its history, the Church has to some degree adapted its practices to those of the cultures it evangelizes. The Church does not deny that there is value in non-Christian religions and philosophies. In his 1981 "Message to the People of Asia," for example, Pope John Paul II wrote:

The Church of Jesus Christ . . . pays homage to the many moral values contained in these religions, as well as to the potential for spiritual living which so deeply marks the traditions and the cultures of whole societies. What seems to bring together and unite, in a particular way, Christians and believers of other religions is an acknowledgment of the need for prayer as an expression of man's spirituality directed towards the Absolute.

Nevertheless, the Church has always taught that other spiritualities inevitably fall short because they do not include Christ, in whom "the whole fullness of deity dwells bodily" and who "is the head of every ruler and authority" (Colossians 2:9–10). In 1975 Pope Paul VI summed up the Church's position:

The Church respects and esteems highly these non-Christian religions, the living expression of the soul of vast groups of people. They carry within them the echo of thousands of years of searching for God, a quest incomplete indeed but often made with great sincerity and righteousness of heart. . . . But neither respect and high esteem for these religions nor the complexity of the theological questions raised is an invitation to the Church to withhold from these non-Christians the proclamation of Jesus Christ. On the contrary, the Church holds that these multitudes have the right to know the riches of the mystery of Christ (see Ephesians 3:8)—riches in which, we believe, the whole humanity can find in unsuspected fullness everything that it is gropingly searching for concerning God, man and his destiny, life and death, and truth (*On Evangelization in the Modern World*, section 53).

A Christian's New Clothes

Questions to Begin

15 minutes
Use a question or two to get warmed up for the reading.

1   Think of a likable mobster in *The Godfather, The Sopranos,* or another gangster show. He loves his family, he goes to church at least twice a year, and he is loyal to his friends. Where did he go wrong? Name some character traits of his that you wouldn't want your children to imitate.

2   What character traits would you find most important in these people? Go down the list quickly, letting group members call out one trait for each person listed. Explain later!
- ❑ neighbor
- ❑ pastor
- ❑ teacher
- ❑ police officer
- ❑ boss
- ❑ coworker
- ❑ employee
- ❑ spouse
- ❑ son or daughter
- ❑ politician
- ❑ doctor
- ❑ lawyer
- ❑ financial adviser

5 minutes
Read the passage aloud. Let individuals take turns reading
paragraphs.

The Reading: Colossians 3:1–17; 4:2–6

Hidden with Christ in God

3:1 So if you have been raised with Christ, seek the things that are above, where Christ is, seated at the right hand of God. 2 Set your minds on things that are above, not on things that are on earth, 3 for you have died, and your life is hidden with Christ in God. 4 When Christ who is your life is revealed, then you also will be revealed with him in glory.

Since You've Stripped Off the Old Life . . .

5 Put to death, therefore, whatever in you is earthly: fornication, impurity, passion, evil desire, and greed (which is idolatry). 6 On account of these the wrath of God is coming on those who are disobedient. 7 These are the ways you also once followed, when you were living that life. 8 But now you must get rid of all such things— anger, wrath, malice, slander, and abusive language from your mouth. 9 Do not lie to one another, seeing that you have stripped off the old self with its practices 10 and have clothed yourselves with the new self, which is being renewed in knowledge according to the image of its creator.

. . . Clothe Yourselves with Christ's Love

11 In that renewal there is no longer Greek and Jew, circumcised and uncircumcised, barbarian, Scythian, slave and free; but Christ is all and in all!
12 As God's chosen ones, holy and beloved, clothe yourselves with compassion, kindness, humility, meekness, and patience. 13 Bear with one another and, if anyone has a complaint against another, forgive each other; just as the Lord has forgiven you, so you also must forgive. 14 Above all, clothe yourselves with love, which binds everything together in perfect harmony. 15 And let the peace of Christ rule in your hearts, to which indeed you were called in the one body. And be thankful. 16 Let the word of Christ dwell in you richly; teach and admonish one another in all wisdom; and with gratitude in your hearts sing psalms, hymns, and spiritual songs to God. 17 And

whatever you do, in word or deed, do everything in the name of the Lord Jesus, giving thanks to God the Father through him. . . .

4:2 Devote yourselves to prayer, keeping alert in it with thanksgiving. 3 At the same time pray for us as well that God will open to us a door for the word, that we may declare the mystery of Christ, for which I am in prison, 4 so that I may reveal it clearly, as I should.

5 Conduct yourselves wisely toward outsiders, making the most of the time. 6 Let your speech always be gracious, seasoned with salt, so that you may know how you ought to answer everyone.

10 minutes
Choose questions according to your interest and time.

1 This reading is full of contrasts. How many can you find?

2 Look at the list of "earthly" practices in 3:5–9. Who is hurt by these actions? Now look at the practices recommended in the rest of the reading. Who is helped by them?

3 Given the behaviors Paul condemns and the ones he recommends, what does he mean by "earthly"? by "things that are above"? How do his meanings differ from our usual ways of using these words?

4 According to this reading, what is the role of gratitude and thanksgiving in a Christian's life?

5 What does Paul say Christ has to do with the way Christians behave?

A Guide to the Reading

If participants have not read this section already, read it aloud. Otherwise go on to "Questions for Application."

S omeone has observed that in the New Testament, the essence of theology is *grace,* and the essence of ethics is *gratitude.* In the first part of his letter to the Colossians, Paul wrote about God's grace in forgiving their sins and giving them a new life in Christ. Now he tells them to be grateful to God while living as new persons in Christ.

3:1–4. "Christ has died, Christ is risen, Christ will come again." When we say this at Mass, do we identify with Christ as Paul does? "You have died," he says, "you have been raised with Christ," and "you also will be revealed with him in glory." Our sins are forgiven, our future is safe with Christ—and meanwhile we have a life to live. Paul, of course, has some advice for us on how to do that.

3:5–10. In last week's reading, we saw how the false teachers were prescribing all kinds of rituals and regulations for character development. Don't believe them, said Paul. We don't grow by going off on our own and following rules but by living as part of Christ's body, the Church. We must hold "fast to the head," Christ himself, and be "held together by its ligaments and sinews" (2:19). We grow by living in love with our fellow Christians.

Once again Paul reminds the Colossians of their baptism. Reading that they have "stripped off the old self" and "clothed [themselves] with the new self," they would remember the night they took off their old clothes and plunged naked into the baptismal waters. When they emerged, dripping and shivering, deacons or deaconesses dressed them in brand-new clothes, the symbol of their new life in Christ. Similarly, Paul says, they must strip off their old ways of living (that's what he means by "whatever . . . is earthly"). Look at his list—every sin on it is an action that harms another person. People who do such things to each other aren't living together in love. They certainly can't help one another to grow in Christ.

3:11–17. Many educators believe that clothes make a big difference in their students' behavior. Nine year olds in blue blazers and plaid skirts are somehow more interested in their schoolwork—and less interested in tormenting one another—than the same kids in shorts and T-shirts. Paul tells the Colossians it's time to put on those new baptismal clothes: that is, it's time to start treating each other with heartfelt kindness.

Like schoolkids in uniforms, newly dressed Christians find their social distinctions breaking down. You, Mr. Christian Slaveowner—your slaves have become your brothers and sisters, and you'd better treat them with respect. And you, Ms. Christian Greek—go ahead and make friends with Ms. Christian Jew and Mr. Christian Barbarian. Christ is in all of you equally. You're all dressed alike.

Kindness—does it seem an odd way to grow in Christ? Would you expect something more difficult, like rigorous diets or special observances? While Christian disciplines can train us to focus on Christ and can help us create new habits, they cannot turn us into the persons we want to become. Only Christ, living in our hearts and in our actions, can do that. To benefit from the forgiveness God offers us, we must forgive one another. To grow in Christ, we must spiritually nourish one another.

4:2–6. Next week we'll look closely at the remaining verses of chapter 3, where Paul spells out ways Christians can nourish one another in everyday life. For now, notice that Paul gives advice not only on living with other Christians but also on relating to people who do not know Christ. Pray that "the mystery of Christ," the truth that Christ is reconciling the entire universe to God, will be proclaimed. Speak graciously to others—about Christ, if appropriate.

Once again Paul tells the Colossians to be grateful, to pray "with thanksgiving." The Greek word used here for thanksgiving is *eucharistía.* Next time you go to Mass, listen to the opening words of the eucharistic prayers. "We come to you, Father, with praise and thanksgiving." "Father, it is our duty and our salvation, always and everywhere to give you thanks." "Father, you are holy indeed, and all creation rightly gives you praise." "Father in heaven, it is right that we should give you thanks and glory." When we gather as Christ's body to commune with Jesus in the Eucharist, we remember God's grace, we respond in gratitude, and we—literally—nourish one another.

Questions for Application

40 minutes
Choose questions according to your interest and time.

1 Reread 3:15–17 and 4:2. What inspires your thanksgiving and gratitude this week?

2 Look at Paul's list of "earthly" actions and attitudes to avoid (3:5–9). In what ways do these behaviors hurt the people who do them? Comment on specific behaviors, not on the whole list. How do these behaviors damage the Church?

3 Now look at Paul's list of actions and attitudes consistent with the "new self" (3:12–17; 4:2–6). How do you feel about being patient with people who are doing the things on Paul's "earthly" list? Is it necessary to bear with them? Do you need to forgive someone? (You might want to keep their name private.) If forgiveness is difficult, where can you find the power to do it?

4 In practical terms, how can you seek or set your mind on "the things that are above"? How can you avoid setting your mind on the actions and attitudes that you'd like to weed out of your life?

5 Are there divisions in your parish that trouble you? Does peace need to be made between any two groups—and if so, can you help to bring it about? Or is an attitude adjustment more to the point— a gut-level recognition that, in spite of the divisions, Christ is in all?

6 How can one manage work, home, friends, and church and still devote oneself to prayer (4:2)? Is it time to examine your priorities?

7 Who are the "outsiders" (4:5) in your life? What questions are they asking (4:6)? What does it mean to make the most of the time, to speak graciously, and to season your words with salt?

For many of us, one of the biggest obstacles to prayer is simply finding the time. Perhaps we should admit that there is no perfect time in our day for prayer and then set a definite time anyway.

George Martin, *Praying with Jesus*

Approach to Prayer

15 minutes
Use this approach—or create your own!

◆ Pray together this prayer traditionally ascribed to St. Francis of Assisi. The person to the left of the leader takes sentence 1. Continue clockwise around the group.

Leader: Let the peace of Christ rule in your hearts.

All: *Lord, make me an instrument of your peace.*

1: Where there is hatred, let me sow love;

2: Where there is injury, pardon;

3: Where there is doubt, faith;

4: Where there is despair, hope;

5: Where there is darkness, light;

6: Where there is sadness, joy.

7: Divine Master, grant that I may not so much seek to be consoled, as to console,

8: To be understood, as to understand,

9: To be loved, as to love,

All: *For it is in giving that we receive;*
It is in pardoning that we are pardoned;
It is in dying that we are born to eternal life.

A Living Tradition

No Free Lunch

This section is a supplement for individual reading.

The moral standards Paul spelled out for Christians went well beyond typical ethics in the Roman Empire. In a time when abortion and infanticide were common, Christians were to nurture all life, born or unborn. While Romans and Greeks assumed that men would have sexual relations with prostitutes, mistresses, and even preadolescent boys, Christian men were to reserve sex for marriage. Unlike their class-conscious neighbors, Christians were to care for the poor, especially widows and orphans; to avoid status seeking and greed; to refrain from anger; to practice hospitality; to serve others irrespective of rank.

Surprisingly, the Church's strictness was probably one reason Christianity attracted so many followers. In *The Rise of Christianity,* sociologist Rodney Stark describes why a faith that makes costly demands is more likely to thrive than a more lenient religion. A permissive religion, Stark writes, tends to attract "free riders"—people who enjoy the group's benefits but have no strong commitment to its purposes. These parasites then weaken the group's values. The group becomes less certain in theology, less enthusiastic in worship, less dedicated to well-doing, and much less attractive to potential converts.

Early Christianity, by contrast, demanded a lot of its members—frequent participation in worship, strict moral discipline, generosity of time and money, and occasionally even imprisonment and execution. The halfhearted quickly lost interest, while dedicated enthusiasts enjoyed the invigorating life of the community. For the truly committed, the new religion offered amazing spiritual benefits: forgiveness of sins, peace with God, the hope of eternal life. It also offered tangible rewards such as health care, respect for women and children, disaster relief, and care for the aged, bereaved, and destitute. The costs of being a Christian were high, but the rewards were worth it. In Stark's words, "Membership in an expensive religion is, for many people, a 'good bargain.' Conventional cost-benefit analysis alone suffices to explain the continued attraction of religions that impose sacrifices and stigmas upon their members."

GOD'S HOUSEHOLD

Questions to Begin

15 minutes
Use a question or two to get warmed up for the reading.

1 If you and the people you live with were stranded on a desert island, who would take charge of what?

2 In what circumstances do you like to give orders? take orders? be your own boss? work with other people?

3 Do opposites attract? Or do birds of a feather flock together? Would you rather spend time with someone very much like you or with someone quite different from you?

5 minutes
*Read the passage aloud. Let individuals take turns reading
paragraphs.*

The Reading: Colossians 3:18–4:1, 7–18

The Household: Life under One Roof

3:18 Wives, be subject to your husbands, as is fitting in the Lord.
19 Husbands, love your wives and never treat them harshly.
20 Children, obey your parents in everything, for this is your
acceptable duty in the Lord. 21 Fathers, do not provoke your children,
or they may lose heart. 22 Slaves, obey your earthly masters in
everything, not only while being watched and in order to please them,
but wholeheartedly, fearing the Lord. 23 Whatever your task, put
yourselves into it, as done for the Lord and not for your masters,
24 since you know that from the Lord you will receive the inheritance
as your reward; you serve the Lord Christ. 25 For the wrongdoer will
be paid back for whatever wrong has been done, and there is no
partiality. 4:1 Masters, treat your slaves justly and fairly, for you know
that you also have a Master in heaven. . . .

The Church: Brothers and Sisters in Christ

7 Tychicus will tell you all the news about me; he is a beloved brother,
a faithful minister, and a fellow servant in the Lord. 8 I have sent him
to you for this very purpose, so that you may know how we are and
that he may encourage your hearts; 9 he is coming with Onesimus, the
faithful and beloved brother, who is one of you. They will tell you
about everything here.
10 Aristarchus my fellow prisoner greets you, as does Mark
the cousin of Barnabas, concerning whom you have received
instructions—if he comes to you, welcome him. 11 And Jesus who is
called Justus greets you. These are the only ones of the circumcision
among my co-workers for the kingdom of God, and they have been a
comfort to me. 12 Epaphras, who is one of you, a servant of Christ
Jesus, greets you. He is always wrestling in his prayers on your behalf,
so that you may stand mature and fully assured in everything that
God wills. 13 For I testify for him that he has worked hard for you
and for those in Laodicea and in Hierapolis. 14 Luke, the beloved
physician, and Demas greet you. 15 Give my greetings to the brothers
and sisters in Laodicea, and to Nympha and the church in her house.
16 And when this letter has been read among you, have it read also in

the church of the Laodiceans; and see that you read also the letter from Laodicea. ¹⁷ And say to Archippus, "See that you complete the task that you have received in the Lord."

¹⁸ I, Paul, write this greeting with my own hand. Remember my chains. Grace be with you.

10 minutes
Choose questions according to your interest and time.

1 In his instructions to the various members of a household, what is Paul trying to accomplish? (Read Ephesians 5:21 for an interesting insight.)

2 Which group addressed in Colossians 3:18–4:1 would find it hardest to follow Paul's directions?

3 In Colossians 4:7–18, Paul mentions a number of Christians by name. Looking at the descriptions, what can you tell about the mix of people among these early Christians?

4 How is Epaphras, the Colossian who brought Christianity to his hometown, similar to his mentor, Paul?

5 Archippus is a member of the church in Colossae. How does Paul's message to Archippus relate to what he has been saying to the Colossians throughout this letter?

A Guide to the Reading

If participants have not read this section already, read it aloud. Otherwise go on to "Questions for Application."

3:18–4:1. This short paragraph has caused a lot of fur to fly. In each of its three household pairs, one person or group is the subordinate (wives, children, slaves); the other is the boss (husbands, fathers, masters). In the first-century Roman household, the boss was always the same person: the paterfamilias, a man with nearly absolute power over his family. For example, a paterfamilias in the Roman Empire had the right to decide whether to bring up, abandon, or kill any infant born in his household. Does this reading mean that it is acceptable to own slaves? In the nineteenth century, some Christians thought so. Does it mean that wives are to obey their husbands? Some Christians still think so. What other options are there?

Lists of household rules were as common two thousand years ago as government regulations are today. Greek philosophers and Jewish writers offered codes of behavior for households, and the New Testament has similar lists in Ephesians, Titus, 1 Timothy, and 1 Peter. Some Scripture scholars point out that the biblical lists differ significantly from the philosophers' lists, which, being based on natural law, assume that the strong will always dominate the weak. By contrast the Christian lists, based on what "is fitting in the Lord," ask those who are strong to practice self-sacrifice on behalf of the weak. In fact, the list in Ephesians 5 begins with a general statement that effectively destroys power relationships altogether: "Be subject to one another out of reverence for Christ" (5:21). Interestingly, the Christian lists are always addressed to the entire congregation. Women, children, and slaves got to listen as the head of the household was ordered to treat them humanely.

Some scholars suggest that the New Testament writers differed from one another on social issues. Paul was a radical: he had a vision that would transform the very roots of society. He described it for the Galatians: "As many of you as were baptized into Christ have clothed yourselves with Christ. There is no longer Jew or Greek, there is no longer slave or free, there is no longer male and female; for all of you are one in Christ Jesus" (3:27–28). The biblical authors who included household codes, by contrast, were more conservative. They chose to stay within the then-accepted social structures—including slavery and patriarchy—but to live by Christian principles of love and service. Now that Western society generally accepts the radical position, we might conclude that the writer of Colossians was, at best, nearsighted. No modern scholar defends slavery, and few defend patriarchal family structures. Nevertheless, we can learn from these household rules. Just as the structures of Roman society were imperfect, so the world today is deeply flawed. Every news report includes examples of injustice, cruelty, and oppression. While we Christians should work for peace and just social structures, how are we to live in the meantime, in the messy circumstances of our lives? Colossians gives us much food for thought and discussion. Whatever we conclude, we must consider this important question: *Why* does the writer suddenly pop this list of rules into this letter? Paul is asking the Colossians to live out Christ's love where it matters most, in everyday relationships.

4:7–18. Paul is getting ready to take the papyrus from his secretary and sign his name to it. First, he sends greetings from his friends. Notice especially the "faithful and beloved brother" Onesimus—he is a slave who used to live in Colossae, and we're going to meet him again next week. Tychicus and Onesimus will personally deliver the letter, and Mark may be coming their direction as well. It looks as if the delegation from Paul will be swinging through nearby Laodicea. "The letter from Laodicea" could also be translated "the letter to Laodicea." There is no longer a letter by either name; some scholars think the letter to the Ephesians was actually a round-robin letter from Ephesus and may be the letter Paul means.

These closing paragraphs show the people of God nourishing one another, not just in their own households or congregations but wherever they are. These "brothers and sisters" have been reconciled to God and to each other through Christ. They are no longer making distinctions based on race, gender, or social status—the list includes Jews and Greeks, slave and free, male and female. "Grace be with you," says Paul. Amazing grace, that brings people of all walks of life together in one family.

Questions for Application

40 minutes
Choose questions according to your interest and time.

1 In this week's selections Paul writes about people who live or work closely together. He is clearly thankful for his coworkers. For whom have you been especially grateful this week?

2 Scripture sometimes calls the Church "the household of God." How should a church be like a household? How should it be different?

3 Everybody is responsible *to* someone—the boss, the board of directors, the shareholders, the electorate. To whom are you responsible? What attitudes should you have toward these people?

4 Most of us are also responsible *for* someone—our employees, our children, our aged parents, other people we care for. How should we as Christians relate to these people?

5 If we see Christ in all the people in our lives, does that change the way we relate to a boss we don't care for, a subordinate who drives us crazy, or a family member who pushes our buttons? How can serving the Lord affect our relationships?

6 Sometimes the appropriate Christian response to someone else is to refuse to do what they ask. When should you as a Christian say no to your boss? to a family member? to someone you are taking care of? What in this week's reading makes you think Paul would agree with you?

7 Paul is surrounded by Christians who "encourage," "greet," "welcome," "comfort," "work hard for," and pray for one another (4:8–13). How do other Christians support you? How can you—individually or as a group—increase networks of mutual support in your parish?

When will any of us reveal our intimate selves to another person? Is it not when we trust the other not to laugh at or scorn or downplay our experience?

William A. Barry, S.J., *Letting God Come Close*

Approach to Prayer

15 minutes
Use one of these approaches—or create your own!

◆ Allow a few moments for silent reflection on beloved family and friends. Participants may then name one or two people for whom they are especially thankful. After each naming, all respond, "Bless [her, him, them], O Lord." End with an Our Father, a Hail Mary, and a Glory to the Father.

◆ Repeatedly Paul says that our relationships are "in the Lord." Thinking of those you love, pray "St. Patrick's Breastplate" in unison:

Christ be with me, Christ before
   me,
Christ be after me, Christ within
   me,
Christ beneath me, Christ above
   me,
Christ at my right hand, Christ at
   my left,
Christ in the fort, Christ in the
   chariot,
Christ in the ship,
Christ in the heart of everyone
   who thinks of me,
Christ in the mouth of everyone
   who speaks to me,
Christ in every eye that sees me,
Christ in every ear that hears me.

A Living Tradition

Walk Right In

This section is a supplement for individual reading.

First-century Christians did not have church buildings. They usually met in homes owned by Christian men or women: Paul mentions Nympha in Laodicea (Colossians 4:15), Philemon in Colossae (Philemon 1), and Prisca and Aquila in Rome (Romans 16:3). These house churches were not exactly like today's Bible-study groups gathered in somebody's family room. The ancient lifestyle was a far cry from modern suburbia's.

Put yourself in Rome or Asia Minor two thousand years ago. If you are a Christian, you probably live in a city. You are probably not rich. If you are free, you may live with your extended family in a one-room apartment with no sanitary or cooking facilities, and probably no windows either, since the street-side rooms in your building are mostly shops. If you are a slave, you live in a fine house—but in the servants' quarters, which are crowded and stuffy. For that matter, even if you are rich you likely sleep in a tiny windowless room. Whatever your status, you have a lot of incentive to get out of bed in the morning!

Fortunately, there are many interesting places to go: the marketplace, public baths, state-owned buildings such as courts, temples, and arenas, and even the homes of your well-to-do neighbors. These homes are quite large, because not only the family but also their business associates, household servants, and some relatives live there. Enclosed rooms around the house's perimeter surround a central space, often open to the sky, that may include rooms or areas for offices, entertainment, libraries, works of art, and places to gather for worship.

It's Saturday night or Sunday morning, and you want to join other Christians to read Scripture, pray, and break bread. You might meet in somebody's room in an apartment building, but that gets crowded pretty fast. You might go to a rented hall, especially if there's a visitor in town and several churches want to hear him speak. Most weeks you will likely go to a house church, a gathering of Christians in one of those houses where you often do business. The entire household has been baptized, and they want you to come. Their door is open. Bring a friend if you like.

A Slave No Longer

Questions to Begin

15 minutes
Use a question or two to get warmed up for the reading.

1 Have you ever intervened in an argument that was none of your business? What happened?

2 What's the best way to persuade someone to do something for you? If you were contacting this person by letter or e-mail, how would you make your case?

5 minutes
Read the passage aloud. Let individuals take turns reading
paragraphs.

The Reading: Philemon 1–25

Greetings to the Church in Your House

1 Paul, a prisoner of Christ Jesus, and Timothy our brother,
    To Philemon our dear friend and co-worker, 2 to Apphia our
sister, to Archippus our fellow soldier, and to the church in your
house:
    3 Grace to you and peace from God our Father and the Lord
Jesus Christ.
    4 When I remember you in my prayers, I always thank my God
5 because I hear of your love for all the saints and your faith toward
the Lord Jesus. 6 I pray that the sharing of your faith may become
effective when you perceive all the good that we may do for Christ.

A Personal Appeal

7 I have indeed received much joy and encouragement from your love,
because the hearts of the saints have been refreshed through you, my
brother.
    8 For this reason, though I am bold enough in Christ to
command you to do your duty, 9 yet I would rather appeal to you on
the basis of love—and I, Paul, do this as an old man, and now also as
a prisoner of Christ Jesus. 10 I am appealing to you for my child,
Onesimus, whose father I have become during my imprisonment.
11 Formerly he was useless to you, but now he is indeed useful* both
to you and to me. 12 I am sending him, that is, my own heart, back to
you. 13 I wanted to keep him with me, so that he might be of service
to me in your place during my imprisonment for the gospel; 14 but I
preferred to do nothing without your consent, in order that your
good deed might be voluntary and not something forced.

From Slave to Brother

15 Perhaps this is the reason he was separated from you for a while,
so that you might have him back forever, 16 no longer as a slave but
more than a slave, a beloved brother—especially to me but how much
more to you, both in the flesh and in the Lord.

*The name Onesimus means "useful" or (compare verse 20) "beneficial."

¹⁷ So if you consider me your partner, welcome him as you would welcome me. ¹⁸ If he has wronged you in any way, or owes you anything, charge that to my account. ¹⁹ I, Paul, am writing this with my own hand: I will repay it. I say nothing about your owing me even your own self. ²⁰ Yes, brother, let me have this benefit from you in the Lord! Refresh my heart in Christ. ²¹ Confident of your obedience, I am writing to you, knowing that you will do even more than I say.

²² One thing more—prepare a guest room for me, for I am hoping through your prayers to be restored to you.

Love, Paul

²³ Epaphras, my fellow prisoner in Christ Jesus, sends greetings to you, ²⁴ and so do Mark, Aristarchus, Demas, and Luke, my fellow workers. ²⁵ The grace of the Lord Jesus Christ be with your spirit.

10 minutes
Choose questions according to your interest and time.

1 Which people mentioned in this letter did you just meet in the letter to the Colossians? What do you know about each of them?

2 What family-relationship terms does Paul use here in speaking to or about Christians?

3 Go through the letter one verse at a time and show what Paul does to persuade Philemon to free Onesimus. For example, in verse 1 he appeals for sympathy—"a prisoner of Christ Jesus," points out that Timothy agrees with him, and acknowledges the strong personal relationship between himself, Timothy, and Philemon. Take it from there!

4 What could Paul mean in verse 19 when he speaks to Philemon about "your owing me even your own self"?

5 In what ways does Paul indicate that he considers Onesimus the slave, Philemon the master, and himself the imprisoned evangelist to be equals?

A Guide to the Reading

If participants have not read this section already, read it aloud. Otherwise go on to "Questions for Application."

1–6. The letter to Philemon is closely related to the letter to the Colossians. If Paul wrote both letters, they may have been written and carried to Colossae at the same time. More likely Colossians was written later, but the cast of characters is the same lovable, faithful bunch. Colossians told them how they ought to think and behave. Philemon lets us see how they actually did.

Philemon is a wealthy homeowner, probably a businessman who met Paul in Ephesus and was converted to Christianity there. Apphia, probably his wife, would have been in charge of the household staff, so this letter is going to concern her. Archippus is a "fellow soldier" in the sense that he too works on behalf of the Christian gospel (Paul singled him out at the end of the letter to the Colossians). He is probably a leader, perhaps a deacon, in the Colossian church. This is a personal letter, but right up front Paul addresses the whole church, a group of Christians who meet in Philemon's house. He is hoping the whole church will join Philemon in welcoming Onesimus, who is carrying the letter.

7–9. In his earlier letters, Paul could sometimes sound impersonal or irritable. Here, by contrast, he is almost touchy-feely. He loves Philemon, his "brother," who has brought him and many others joy, encouragement, and refreshment. Numerous stints in prison along with the aches and pains of old age may have mellowed Paul. (The word he uses for "old man" commonly applied to men aged 50 to 56!)

10–14. Paul also loves his "child," Onesimus, who has become a Christian because of his contact with Paul. The name *Onesimus,* which means "useful" or "profitable," was commonly and optimistically given to slaves. Here it inspires in Paul a burst of punning. If Philemon laughed at the puns, it must have been in spite of himself. Onesimus had been a problem employee—a thief or embezzler, or perhaps just a bad manager. Philemon could not have been entirely happy to see him. *Send him back? Why not just keep him?* Philemon may have thought. *But wait—how can you identify him with me? He can hardly serve in my place. I have money; I can help support Paul. What can my least-effective employee do? What is this good deed Paul wants from me?*

15–19. Paul has already said he is Philemon's brother and Onesimus's father. Now he says he is Onesimus's brother, and Onesimus is Philemon's brother. He has said Onesimus can serve him in place of Philemon; now he asks Philemon to welcome Onesimus in place of Paul and promises that Paul will pay what Onesimus owes (though Philemon owes Paul more than Onesimus owes Philemon—that is, Philemon is a Christian because of Paul). Don't bother making a diagram. The explanation is simple: we are all "brothers and sisters in Christ" (Colossians 1:2).

20–22. "So, my brother, just do it," says Paul. "Do even more than I say." The traditional story is that Onesimus is a runaway slave who meets Paul, converts to Christianity, returns home, and is freed by Philemon. Some scholars tell the story differently: Onesimus and Philemon have a serious falling-out, Onesimus asks Paul to mediate, and Philemon agrees to give Onesimus a second chance. In either case, Paul does not ask Philemon to free Onesimus, nor does he command Philemon to send Onesimus back to him. He leaves Philemon's response entirely up to him—though of course the entire church is watching to see what he will do. And then Paul adds (is this subtle pressure?) that he hopes to come and visit!

23–25. Paul sends greetings from five men we already met in Colossians, prominent Christians all. There are traditions about what happened to these men: Epaphras became bishop of Colossae and was martyred; Mark wrote the second Gospel and was martyred; Aristarchus became bishop of Thessalonica and was martyred; Demas deserted Paul and became a pagan priest; Luke wrote the third Gospel and the Acts of the Apostles and may have died of old age. What happened to Onesimus? Nobody knows for sure. Certainly Philemon took Paul's advice and began treating him as a brother; otherwise his story would not have been saved for posterity. According to some traditions, Onesimus eventually became a bishop. As for Paul, he continued bouncing from one hardship to another and was eventually beheaded in Rome. He never made it to Philemon's guest room.

Questions for Application

40 minutes
Choose questions according to your interest and time.

1 Reread verses 4–5 and 7. Once again, what are you especially thankful for this week? What can you do to keep a spirit of gratitude in your life? How can you remind yourself to be thankful?

2 When you want someone to do something for you, how do you get their cooperation? When is an order necessary? When is it counterproductive? In Scripture, God both commands and invites. Which way do you tend to think of God? Is your picture of God balanced?

3 In verses 15–16, Paul says there may have been a reason for the separation between Philemon and Onesimus. In your life, has a bad situation ever led to good results? Could you have had the same results without going through the difficult time?

4 We live in an individualistic age, and it's easy to forget that we Christians are here for each other. What would have happened to Onesimus if he had tried to solve his problem with Philemon on his own? Are there situations in your life that would be easier to face if somebody stood alongside you? Are you willing to come to someone else's aid?

5 Philemon had opened his house to the entire church at Colossae, and Paul felt comfortable asking for the guest room. Is it necessary to have a large house in order to be hospitable? In what ways do you show hospitality? When do people need hospitality the most? How could you— individually or as a group— reach out to them?

I believe that a group's prayer, just like an individual's prayer, that does not lead to outreach, according to the proper vocations of the members, is suspect.

M. Basil Pennington, *Centered Living*

Approach to Prayer

15 minutes
Use this approach—or create your own!

◆ The leader begins by reading Colossians 3:13. During a few moments of silence, think of people in your life whom you need to forgive. Then turn your thoughts to people who have forgiven you. Give thanks for them, silently or aloud. When the leader signals that it is time to close, let a participant read this prayer by Christina Rossetti:

O Lord Jesus,
because, being full of foolishness,
     we often sin and have to
     ask pardon,
help us to forgive as we would be
     forgiven,
neither mentioning old offenses
     committed against us,
nor dwelling upon them in
     thought,
nor being influenced by them in
     heart;
but loving each other freely, as
     you freely love us;
for your name's sake.
Amen.

Before saying good-bye, join hands in a circle and pray the Our Father.

A Living Tradition

New Best Friends

This section is a supplement for individual reading.

In A.D. 203 in Carthage, North Africa, four brand-new Christians shared the kiss of peace and waited calmly for the slash of a gladiator's sword. Perpetua was a noblewoman. Saturninus was probably of lower rank. Revocatus and Felicity were slaves. Under the circumstances, social status was not uppermost in their minds.

Although Christianity was illegal in the Roman Empire until the fourth century, officials usually turned a blind eye to it. Now and then, however, some administrator would get tough—usually for political reasons—and harass a few dissidents. Carthage in 203 was getting dangerous for Christians, and Perpetua's father was heartbroken when his only daughter, just twenty-two years old and a new mother, was arrested for her decision to become a follower of Christ. He pleaded, then threatened, and finally refused to see her, to no avail. Perpetua and her companions were baptized anyway, and then tossed into a dungeon to await sentencing. After many weeks the date was set: they would face wild animals in Carthage's amphitheater. The young noblewoman and her friends, consoled by visions of heaven, prepared to die.

Meanwhile the slave Felicity, now eight months pregnant, was frightened. It was against Roman law to kill a pregnant woman. She feared being left behind when her friends were killed, only to be executed later among strangers. Her companions shared her concern. As brothers and sisters in Christ, they wanted to go through their entire ordeal together. Three days before the exhibition, the condemned Christians prayed earnestly for Felicity. Immediately she went into labor and gave birth to a daughter, who was given to a Christian woman to raise.

Perpetua herself left a stirring written account of the young Christians' imprisonment, and another Christian described their martyrdom. The men were attacked by a leopard, a bear, and a wild boar; the two young mothers were gored by an enraged cow. Finally, after the crowd had their fill of excitement, gladiators stabbed the four companions to death. Together to the end, they lived by St. Paul's description: among those who are baptized in Christ, "there is no longer slave or free, there is no longer male and female; for all of you are one in Christ Jesus" (Galatians 3:28).

Truly God, Truly Human

Most of us have been baptized Christians for as long as we can remember. We live in a country where more than 80 percent of the people identify themselves as Christians. We hear people praise Christian values. And at Christmas and Easter, when we are not distracted by reindeers and bunnies, we are used to singing about a baby who was worshiped and a man who rose from the dead. The belief that Jesus is God is not shocking. For many of us, it's even harder to believe he was a man who sweated, got tired, and sometimes came down with a cold.

The Colossians had quite a different perspective. Even though they had not met Jesus, they had a fair idea of what he looked like—they knew other Jewish people from Palestine, and they may have met some of his relatives or close friends. His appearance was ordinary, but the stories circulating about him were amazing. He had healed people, fed huge crowds out of a boy's lunch, changed the weather. After a brutal and unfair execution, he had come back from the dead (no doubt some of their neighbors dismissed these reports as we do today with "Elvis sightings"). They believed he was the Messiah, the liberator, and they had joined the small group dedicated to following him. But they thought of him basically as an extraordinary man, not as Lord of the cosmos, and they didn't see why he should mind if they listened to other interesting religious teachers as well.

The Colossians did not read from the Gospels every Sunday—the Gospels had not yet been written. They did not say the Nicene Creed, which proclaims that Jesus is "God from God, . . . one in Being with the Father," for it would not be written for centuries. They were used to saying "Jesus is Lord," but they did not fully understand that Jesus is God. Yet until the Colossians understood that Christ, and Christ alone, had forgiven their sins, freed them from slavery to sinister powers, and given them new life, they were in danger of losing their faith altogether.

Paul wrote to help the Colossians—and other Christians interested in customizing their Christianity with imported spiritual practices—to see the unique nature of the Christ they followed. The Christ he reveals is far more than a local guru with strange powers and interesting insights; he is creator and ruler of the entire universe. And even though Paul does not come right out and tell the Colossians that Jesus equals God, what else could they think after reading what Paul says about him?

♦ Christ is the image of the invisible God.
♦ Christ is before all things.
♦ All things were created through Christ and for Christ.
♦ In Christ all the fullness of God was pleased to dwell.
♦ Christ has reconciled to God you who were once estranged.
♦ Christ in you is the hope of glory.
♦ In Christ are hidden all the treasures of wisdom and knowledge.
♦ Christ is the head of every ruler and authority.
♦ Christ is seated at the right hand of God.

The description of Christ in the letter to the Colossians helped guide the young Christian Church over the next four centuries as it struggled to understand its Lord. In what ways is Jesus a human being? In what ways is he divine? How does his divinity relate to his humanity? Across the Roman Empire bishops and theologians argued passionately over these issues. The Church's eventual conclusion, however, is clear. In A.D. 451, the Council of Chalcedon issued the definition that has been the standard of Christian teaching ever since. "Our Lord Jesus Christ [is] one and the same [person], at once complete in Godhead and complete in manhood, truly God and truly man, . . . in two natures, without confusion, without change, without division, without separation."

This God/man, Jesus, is ruler of the universe, and no other powers, natural or supernatural, begin to compare with him. He is also head of the Church, and in him we enjoy renewed relationships with God and with each other. Whenever we pause and think of our personal connection to the loving Power who hung the stars and directs the tides, what can we do but give thanks?

The Slavery Question

Philemon, a prominent Christian, owned slaves. Paul did not tell him that slavery is wrong. Why not? Several times New Testament authors offer rules for how slaves and, occasionally, slaveholders should behave (1 Corinthians 7:20–24; Ephesians 6:5–9; Colossians 3:22–4:1; 1 Timothy 6:1–2; Titus 2:9–10; 1 Peter 2:18–20). Never does anyone suggest that slavery should be abolished. Why not?

Before addressing these questions, most modern writers point out that slavery in the Roman Empire was different from slavery in the American South. In the first century A.D., slavery was not based on race. Though slave traders existed, most slaves came from other sources: some were war captives, some sold themselves (or were sold by their fathers) in order to pay debts, some were born into slavery. Some slaves held highly responsible positions as administrators, bankers, shopkeepers, and teachers.

On the other hand, slaves who worked in mines or rowed boats or constructed buildings or farmed were regularly overworked, underfed, poorly housed, and beaten. Women and young boys and girls were often victims of sexual abuse. Slaves were not permitted to marry without their owner's permission, and families could be broken up at the master's whim. Children of a slave mother were automatically slaves themselves, and many slave women were bred to provide more slaves for the household or the slave market. Some masters were sadistic, and their slaves were helpless to resist them: Seneca tells of a slave owner named Vedius Pollio who threw slaves who annoyed him into a pond full of man-eating lampreys.

Naturally slaves frequently ran away, escaping into the anonymity of large cities. If a runaway slave was caught, however, he or she could legally be "scourged, branded, mutilated, or fitted with a metal collar, perhaps even be crucified, thrown to beasts, or killed," according to New Testament scholar Joseph Fitzmyer. Not until the second century did the empire outlaw capital punishment for escaped slaves.

Clearly slavery, in the Roman Empire as in America, was evil. So why didn't the early Christians protest, lead revolts, try to outlaw this dehumanizing system?

Though there is no record of any Christian antislavery protests in the Roman Empire, Christians were proclaiming ideals that, when put into practice, eventually made slavery unthinkable. Scripture repeatedly asserts that the distinction between slave and free is irrelevant in Christ. Slaveholders and slaves mingled at Christian worship meetings and called one another "brother" and "sister." In principle, at least, the slave of a Christian master was far better off than other slaves. Nevertheless, Christians continued to hold slaves.

Maybe Christians didn't fight the system because they found the task impossibly huge. The economy of the entire empire was built on slave labor. One third of the population was enslaved; in fact, a lot of Christians were slaves themselves. Slave revolts were common enough, but they were usually ruthlessly crushed. What good would it do to start another one?

Perhaps Christians didn't protest slavery because reforming governments was not a priority for them. For one thing, few Christians had any political power. For another, first-century Christians thought Christ would return at any moment. If the world as we know it is doomed and God's glorious kingdom is just around the corner, why try to change mere earthly power structures? Isn't it more important to tell people to get ready to meet Jesus?

Or maybe Christians didn't object to slavery as an institution because they could not imagine an alternative. Slavery was so much a part of their environment that they never thought to question it. Humanize it, yes: Christian slaveholders were repeatedly told to treat their slaves with dignity. But free the whole lot of them? Who would do the work?

It is sad but true, as New Testament scholars Carolyn Osiek and David L. Balch point out, that "not until after the Industrial Revolution produced machines that could do much of the work formerly done by slaves did moralists raise serious questions about the institution of slavery itself, and only then did French and American abolitionists reject it." It makes one wonder—what abuses in today's world seem as normal to us as water to a fish? Are our eyes closed to injustices that will seem painfully obvious to future generations?

L ike a camping trip, a Bible discussion group works best if you agree on where you're going and how you intend to get there. Many groups use their first meeting to talk over such questions and reach a consensus. Here is a checklist of issues, with bits of advice from people who have experience in Bible discussions. (A planning discussion will go more smoothly if the leaders have thought through the following issues beforehand.)

Agree on your purpose. Are you getting together to gain wisdom and direction for your lives? to finally get acquainted with the Bible? to support one another in following Christ? to encourage those who are exploring—or reexploring—the Church? for other reasons?

Agree on attitudes. For example: "We're all beginners here." "We're here to help one another understand and respond to God's word." "We're not here to offer counseling or direction to one another." "We want to read Scripture prayerfully." What do *you* wish to emphasize? Make it explicit!

Agree on ground rules. Barbara J. Fleischer, in her useful book *Facilitating for Growth,* recommends that a group clearly state its approach to the following:

- ◆ *Preparation.* Do we agree to read the material and prepare answers to the questions before each meeting?
- ◆ *Attendance.* What kind of priority will we give to our meetings?
- ◆ *Self-revelation.* Are we willing to help the others in the group gradually get to know us—our weaknesses as well as our strengths, our needs as well as our gifts?
- ◆ *Listening.* Will we commit ourselves to listening to one another?
- ◆ *Confidentiality.* Will we keep everything that is shared *with* the group *in* the group?
- ◆ *Discretion.* Will we refrain from sharing about the faults and sins of people who are not in the group?
- ◆ *Encouragement and support.* Will we give as well as receive?
- ◆ *Participation.* Will we give each person the time and opportunity to make a contribution?

You could probably take a pen and draw a circle around *listening* and *confidentiality.* Those two points are especially important.

The following items could be added to Fleischer's list:

◆ *Relationship with parish.* Is our group part of the adult faith-formation program? independent but operating with the express approval of the pastor? not a parish-based group?

◆ *New members.* Will we let new members join us once we have begun the six weeks of discussions?

Agree on housekeeping.

◆ *When will we meet?*

◆ *How often will we meet?* Meeting weekly or every other week is best if you can manage it. William Riley remarks, "Meetings once a month are too distant from each other for the threads of the last session not to be lost" *(The Bible Study Group: An Owner's Manual).*

◆ *How long will meetings run?*

◆ *Where will we meet?*

◆ *Is any setup needed?* Christine Dodd writes that "the problem with meeting in a place like a church hall is that it can be very soul-destroying," given the cold, impersonal feel of many church facilities. If you have to meet in a church facility, Dodd recommends doing something to make the area homey *(Making Scripture Work).*

◆ *Who will host the meetings?* Leaders and hosts are not necessarily the same people.

◆ *Will we have refreshments?* Who will provide them? Don Cousins and Judson Poling make this recommendation: "Serve refreshments if you like, but save snacks and other foods for the end of the meeting to minimize distractions" (Leader's Guide 1).

◆ *What about child care?* Most experienced leaders of Bible discussion groups discourage bringing infants or other children to adult Bible discussions.

Agree on leadership. You need someone to facilitate—
to keep the discussion on track, to see that everyone has a chance

to speak, to help the group stay on schedule. Rena Duff, editor of the newsletter *Sharing God's Word Today,* recommends having two or three people take turns leading the discussions.

It's okay if the leader is not an expert on the Bible. You have this booklet, and if questions come up that no one can answer, you can delegate a participant to do a little research between meetings. It's important for the leader to set an example of listening, to draw out the quieter members (and occasionally restrain the more vocal ones), to move the group on when it gets stuck, to remind the members of their agreements, and to summarize what the group is accomplishing.

Bible discussion is an opportunity to experience the fulfillment of Jesus' promise "Where two or three are gathered in my name, I am there among them" (Matthew 18:20). Put your discussion group in Jesus' hands. Pray for the guidance of the Spirit. And have a great time exploring God's word together!

Y ou can use this booklet just as well for individual study as for group discussion. While discussing the Bible with other people can be a rich experience, there are advantages to reading on your own. For example:

◆ You can focus on the points that interest you most.

◆ You can go at your own pace.

◆ You can be completely relaxed and unashamedly honest in your answers to all the questions, since you don't have to share them with anyone!

My suggestions for using this booklet on your own are these:

◆ Don't skip the Questions to Begin. The questions can help you as an individual reader warm up to the topic of the reading.

◆ Take your time on the Questions for Careful Reading and Questions for Application. While a group will probably not have enough time to work on all the questions, you can allow yourself the time to consider all of them if you are using the booklet by yourself.

◆ After reading the Guide to the Reading, go back and reread the Scripture text before answering the Questions for Application.

◆ Take the time to look up all the parenthetical Scripture references.

◆ Since you control the pace, give yourself plenty of opportunities to reflect on the meaning of Colossians and Philemon for you. Let your reading be an opportunity for these words to become God's words to you.

Bibles

The following editions of the Bible contain the full set of biblical books recognized by the Catholic Church, along with a great deal of useful explanatory material:
- The Catholic Study Bible (Oxford University Press), which uses the text of the New American Bible
- The Catholic Bible: Personal Study Edition (Oxford University Press), which also uses the text of the New American Bible
- The New Jerusalem Bible, the regular or standard (not the reader's) edition (Doubleday)

Books

- Joseph A. Fitzmyer, *The Letter to Philemon: A New Translation with Introduction and Commentary* (New York: Doubleday, 2000).
- Carolyn Osiek and David L. Balch, *Families in the New Testament World: Households and House Churches,* The Family, Religion, and Culture (Louisville, Ky.: Westminster John Knox Press, 1997).
- Rodney Stark, *The Rise of Christianity: How the Obscure, Marginal Jesus Movement Became the Dominant Religious Force in the Western World in a Few Centuries* (San Francisco: HarperSanFrancisco, 1997).
- N. T. Wright, *The Epistles of Paul to the Colossians and to Philemon: An Introduction and Commentary* (Grand Rapids, Mich.: W. B. Eerdmans, 1986).

How has Scripture had an impact on your life? Was this booklet helpful to you in your study of the Bible? Please send comments, suggestions, and personal experiences to Kevin Perrotta, General Editor, Trade Editorial Department, Loyola Press, 3441 N. Ashland Ave., Chicago, IL 60657.